Untitled

Copyright © 2025 by Lance Robert Jr.

All rights reserved. No portion of this book may be reproduced in any form without written permission from the publisher or author, except as permitted by U.S. copyright law.

Cover: *Lance Robert Jr. at Age Seven*, painted by Sheri Robert

Roar Publishing

roarpublishing.org

ISBN: 979-8-9989991-0-9

LCCN: 2025910484

Untitled

A Book of Poems

By Lance Robert Jr.

Roar Publishing

In loving memory of Peter Summers Anderson, my late grandfather.

Contents

Preface xiii

Untitled

Untitled 3

Powerful 4

Disenchantment 5

Confusion 6

Unrequited 7

Still 8

Why? 9

Because. 10

Dreamy 11

Frustrated 12

Friend 14

Happier 15

Invisible 16

Bittersweet 17

Beast 18

Change 19

Insufferable	20
Flame	21
Feelings	23
Letter	25
Hurricane	26
Mom!	27
Sheesh!	29
Sometimes	30
Stream	31
Forgot	32
Drama	34
Success	36
Future	38
Grandmother	39
School	40
Oops	41
Graduation	42
Rubicon	44
Broken	45
Mother	47

Feeling	49
Metamorphosis	50
Tell Me What I Need To Know Suite	
A Better Place	53
Tell Me What I Need To Know	55

Preface

Some things are best left untitled, and if anything, the teenage experience is an unrivaled proof of this notion. The so-called "wonder years" are different for everyone and cannot be comfortably homogenized under one title. At the same time, everyone's teenage experience is alike in one regard: it is a time of change. It is that awkward period between childhood and adulthood in which one strives to answer a simple yet mind-boggling question: Why? Why am I here? Who am I, and what was I put on Earth to do? This is precisely why the years of passion and puberty cannot be titled. They are a reckoning with the name given to us as babies and the name we choose for ourselves as full citizens of this oblate spheroid we call home. As such, there is no name we adolescents can claim—hence the title of this coming-of-age book of poems: *Untitled*.

    There's one more reason I mustered the audacity to title this book *Untitled*. I wrote my first poem at the age of three. It was a freestyle, lasting ten minutes at the least. My Mom was lucky to have noticed my lyrical dance in its last quarter, and caught an abridged version, albeit with all but 4 gigabytes of ram on her 2012 clink-clank computer. After all these years, I never officially titled the poem. It sits as the first entry in this book, sharing a title, or lack of one, with the overall project, *Untitled*.

  Well, ok. Perhaps there's one final reason this book bears no title. My grandfather passed away unexpectedly on December 27, 2024. He was a poet and musician—a really good one, at that. A Vietnam War veteran with PTSD, he lived in a fantasy world. He spoke of national recognition, touring the hottest spots with his very own band, and whisking away to the Land of Oz or wherever else by way of his ruby red slippers (that were actually gray—just red in spirit). I spoke with him every Sunday, and he always talked about how much joy I brought him and about how much I reminded him of his teenage self. It wasn't until recently that I figured out what it all meant.

  My grandfather was called home before he could bring to fruition the high life he spoke of. But maybe, in reality, he'd never planned to do any of that stuff. Maybe the hour-long fantasies he'd share with me over the phone weren't for himself, but for me. Perhaps he said all that to inspire me—to let me know, without expressly telling me, that he wanted his dreams to live through me. Perhaps I am the realization of his fantasies. It is this spiritual passage of responsibility—this heirloom of my grandfather's and all other ancestors' dreams that I cannot give a name. It is too great a responsibility and too high a calling to injustice with mere words.

The last section of this book is a tribute to my grandfather, entitled "Tell Me What I Need To Know Suite," after his most iconic catchphrase. Leading up to it is my rendition of the entirety of my experience as a teenager, from parents to friends to crushes to anxiety, frustration, joy, and everything in between. I thank you endlessly, dear reader, and I hope you have as much fun reading this as I had writing it.

— Lance Robert Jr.
April 2025

Untitled

Untitled

I am not just a God lover.
I am not just a corn eater.
I am not just a wisher on dandelions.
I am not just a strawberry milk drinker.

I am a rocket that blasts off into space.

I am not just a dog feeder.
I am not just a chicken eater.
I am not just Mommy's student.
I am not just a player with Legos at Granny's house.

Oh, yeah, oh yeah.

One...two...three...blast off!

I am a rocket that blasts off into space.

(I wrote this when I was three)

Powerful

Out of the mouths of the mute came the loudest cry.
The hippopotami
Learned to fly,
Then, the pigs followed suit.
The spider squished the man under its eight giant boots.
The moon told the sun it was her time to shine.
The linear function stepped out of line.

The mockingbird found his own song to sing,
And they say that hope ain't a powerful thing!

Disenchantment

Cancer and Scorpio danced in the midnight sky,
Said, "Hi!"
To Gemini
Walking by,
And as I closed by eyes
I began to fly
Free
Among the stars I'd animated;

Before your body's been chained,
It's easy to let your soul be emancipated.

In daylight dreams, I reveled in the clouds;
Nothing was impossible when my imagination was too loud
For me to hearken unto worries and strife.
Ye, when once I dreamed of the extraordinary
I dream now of a normal life.

Confusion

I want to learn—
I want to grow—
But unfortunately,
That's all I know.
"I'm meant for more!" and such and such,
But as for what, I couldn't tell you much.
In truth, I'm not quite sure what I want,
And I don't quite want to be sure
That what I want is what I need—
That what I want is able to feed—
A family.
That what I want is able to seed
A child—and sprout for him a life worth living.
Is that what I live for—
To spread my DNA?
Is that what I desire—
For my presence on this Earth not to pass away?

Perhaps I'll stop pondering what I want
As to not blind myself to what I'm meant to be,
When what I'm meant for is not defined
By what I see when I look at me.

Unrequited

When I saw her walking by, my eyes popped out;
My pituitary gland began to scream and shout.
One glimpse was enough for my puberted mind
To put all other cares behind.

But I must've gotten lost in a mindless stare,
For she herself was made aware,

"Do I know you?" she asked of me.

"Uh, no! I'm just staring at that tree!"

Welp, there's another love gone bleak
For only the seventh time this week.

Still

I don't always laugh at your jokes,
But I still deserve a seat at the table.
I don't walk quite like you—
I don't talk quite like you—
But I still deserve a seat at the table.

Sometimes I make choices you don't agree with,
But I still deserve a seat at the table.
I don't think quite like you—
I don't act quite like you—
But I still deserve a seat at the table.

We are not a lot alike,
But I still deserve a seat at the table.
I don't look quite like you—
I don't live quite like you—
But I still deserve a seat at the table.

Why?

"I'll do it later," some kid said to himself,
"For later's when I do my best work."
And that kid's book
Sat on its shelf
'Till 11:59 began to lurk.

"I don't wanna do it," another kid said.
"For there's just too much on my plate"
And that little girl
Sat on her bed
'Till she had to turn it in late.

Why is it that we procrastinate?

Because.

I think I know.
I have the answer to the question posed a poem ago.
We put things off because we fear
We are not able.
How can we act when we give our acts the label
That they're not good enough?

Thus, my friend, I tell you kind
To put perfection second to peace of mind
And then you will find
That daunting task a lot less crazy.

Now I would tell you more but—
Eh—
I'm too lazy.

Dreamy

The ladies were after me today;
When I walked by, they looked my way.

I strutted downtown to the city square,
Met with "Oos" and "Awes" as I flipped my hair,
And I approached a group of girlies gathered there.

"Where've you been all my life—just where, oh where?"
Said each of them at the exact same time.
I responded, "Ladies, please, just wait in line!"

We walked for a block, and as they told me I was fine,
We passed by a clock reading 9:59,
But then an alarm began to scream at ten.
Dang it!
It was a dream again.

Frustrated

I've pent up my frustration
And I don't know what to do with it.
I've been giving, giving, giving
But these people got me achin'
And I'm forgetting what's the use of it.

I'm starting to think I should teach 'em a lesson—
Give 'em what they've been asking for—
For if I'm to make just one confession,
I've got a whole lotta smoke,
And I'm no longer quite sure what I'm masking it for

I was hounded yesterday like a beagle,
But—Oh!—next time won't be the same!
Cuz I've been thinking of a response
And little they know, I'm hard like an eagle
Who's not willing to play that game.

Hmm.

Or maybe I choose to play the game
When I choose to respond.
Perhaps I'll choose to let it go—
To keep this tiger tame—

Cuz their opinion isn't worth a dime
And utterly, they're not worth my time.

Friend

My ride or die
My twin, my friend
My "I'll be with you 'till the end"
My "All I want is the best for you"
My "Whatever you need from me, I'll do"
My ace, my boy
My cheer and joy
My—oh my—what would I do
If it weren't for a friend like you?

Happier

You were just here, and now you're gone.
You were my solid ground—my lawn—
As in you were my foundation,
But now my tears are libation,
Poured out that one day we might meet again—
Not right here, but in another land.
So I'll wipe my tears and clear the air
Cuz I know you're happier there.

Invisible

I'm the invisible man.

When I walk by
No one says "Hi."

I'm never celebrated,
However, hardly am I ever abhored;

In all, I'm frankly just ignored.

When I act out
I'm never congratulated—
Nor indicted—
And when there are parties
I'm never invited.

Boy, have they some nerve to treat me like they treat me!
But that's okay;
They just can't see me like I see me.

Bittersweet

Are you really sweet,
Or is it a performance?
Does what's beneath that caramelized crust
Warrant abhorrence?

Why is it always the ones who
Smell so,
Taste so,
Look so good

Who hide a wretched demon
Under the hood
Of a confection?

Where sourced is your affection?

From the mountains of sincerity,
Or rivers of deception?

Beast

Pimples popping up and down like whack-a-mole—
Hormones popping off like Jack-of-all
Trades—

It invades
Like Alexander;
I can't meander
With puberty on the prowl.
These girls are running through my mind—
My body's smelling foul.

Voice is cracking;
Cares are lacking;

It's attacking
My life and my peace—

I say all this to say that
Puberty's a beast!

Change

I don't wanna grow up.

I mean, I used to want to grow up,
But that was back when I had a whole childhood ahead of me.
Now, I'm practically at the end of it,
And it's hard knowing change is soon to come.

But that's what they say, isn't it?
"Change is the only constant in life"...or something?

So I guess there's no use moping around about it,
And I'm gonna have to embrace it eventually,

But until then,

I'm gonna live in the present;
I'm gonna be a kid.

And I think when change comes knocking at my door

I'll be ready.

Insufferable

No man is an island,
Entire of itself,

But some are peninsulas.

Flame

Tolerance is great,
But love is higher.
Where tolerance is the absence of hate,
Love is the intent to inspire.

What emotion could the phrase "I tolerate you."
Possibly more evoke than "I love you."
But cold-heartedness
And contempt?

Where you find hate,
Don't just refuse to participate—
Resist it—
For compliance and complacency are sins the same;

If that woman's identity is stolen,
Call her by name;

And if that child's heart is yearning,
Love him without shame.

Where tolerance is a heap of charcoal
Without passion to claim,

Love is
A flame.

Feelings

"Hey, man!"

"Hey."

"How are you?"

"I'm okay."

"You're sitting alone. I know that's not true."

"I don't mind—it doesn't matter—what's the matter with you?"

"Let's talk about our feelings."

"Talk about our feelings? You know that's not what men do."

"I do. But don't men have feelings too?"

"I don't feel like talking, bro."

"And you don't have to, you know—just know that sometimes voicing them can let your feelings go."

"Hmm. If you say so."

"But if you need some space, I can leave and let you rest.

"Uh, yeah, maybe that'd be best."

"All good, man—all cool. That's a step in healing."

...

"WAIT! Wait up, bro. Let's talk about our feelings."

Letter

Dear Humankind,

My name is Dandelion, and my brother's Mr. Weed,
And I'm writing this to let you know
That on behalf of all plantkind, we are dispersing our seeds
That our kingdom may rise and overgrow!

You have uprooted our brethren and leeched our soils,
And with every wretched plan
You have rotten our fruits—left us to spoil—
Therefore, we are taking back our land!

The movement started small—
A flower in the concrete—
But now, like redwoods, it's grown all too tall—
Every backyard and every city street—

Vegetation shall devour!

Insincerely,

Dandelion Flower

Hurricane

There's a hurricane in town,
And I'm in the eye;

When it comes to being busy,
Boy, am I
A lucky guy!

I've got to be here,
And I've got to be there.

I've got stuff to do then
And stuff to do now.

I've got work for this class,
And it's starting to amass.

I don't mean to be crass,
But junior year is kicking my...

Gluteus maximus.

Mom!

"Hey, son!

Who are you texting?
I wanna know her name.

Hey, kid!

I need to de-stress—
Help me download this game.

Hey, dude!

Can you grab your Mamma a pop?

Hey—what's your name again?

You're trying your best to annoy me—
Please stop.

Hey, lil' boy!

Don't you have homework to do?

Hey, Boo Boo!

Good luck on that test—
Make sure you pray.

Hey, baby!

Have I told you I love you today?"

"Yes, Mom!"

Sheesh!

Sheesh!

Girl, you're so bright!
When you walk by, I lose my appetite,
Cuz there's nothing in which I'd rather delight
Than your eyes
And your smile.
I try to keep composure—
Try not to stare at you a while—
But I just can't hang cuz I'm addicted to your style.

Sheesh!

Girl, I've got it bad for you.
The way that hair coils 'round the backdrop of that chiseled face—
The way those eyes transport me to a place
That these weary feet long ache to grace—
Nobody gets me going like you do—you occupy that niche;
Baby, I've got way too much to say so I've gotta just say

Sheesh!

Sometimes

Sometimes I hate my life
Because sometimes I forget
That amazing thing life brought me the other day.

Sometimes I hate myself
Because sometimes I forget
That amazing thing I did the other day.

Sometimes I am doubtful
Because sometimes I forget
The people in my circle who trusted me when I didn't trust myself.

Sometimes I am complacent
Because sometimes I forget
I'm meant for more.

Stream

Yesterday I came upon a stream
And rested by the water's edge,
And as I rose from wild dreams
My eyes did tear apart the seams
Of my imagination,

For in the water lied a man
Whom I don't see when I fall asleep;

In the water lied a man
Who was not who I thought him to be.

Who was he?

He was the harsh reality
Reflecting back at weary me.

Forgot

Hey girl,

Did I mention that I saved that cat from a tree?
Donated a few million to the treasury?

Won 20 tournaments in D1 basketball?
And that I'm 6 feet and 6 inches tall?

Or what about the time I ran for president?
The time I went to Buckingham Palace and became a resident?

Did I tell you 'bout the fact that I founded 27 non-profit organizations?
Or 'bout how all the celebrities I know call me the greatest in the nation?

So, you're impressed?

Yeah, I get that a lot.

But you don't think I'm being honest?

Oh! I almost forgot:

Did I tell you about that fire-breathing dragon I fought?

Drama

I'm a poet,
And so's my Mamma;

Therefore sometimes we get into poetic drama.

I asked of her,
"Mom, would you please? You're getting on my nerves;
The way you treat me is something nobody deserves!"

She replied,
"Boy, sweeten that attitude cuz it's sour like lime,
And I know you know 'fought' and 'forgot' don't rhyme!"

"That's it, Mom—you're going in my book!
Remember that I can use free verse to portray you as a crook!"

"Son, dear son—you better not shout!
For I can use Iambic Pentameter to curse you out without cursing you out!"

And so continues the poetic drama!
Though we may tussle—
Over where to place that comma—
I just wanna say that
I love you, Mamma!

Success

When you really want something
You don't think about what it takes;
When you really love somebody
You don't care about the aches,
Compromises, sacrifices, nor stakes.

You've no need for motivation
To get these things done—
No "why?", no "how?"—
It's kinda just...fun!

Yes, success
Is stress, but
Also the relentless will to invest—
Not in a calculated outcome
Nor an arbitrary date—
But a dream that seeks a fight with fate!

Success is not a function
But a crazy scatterplot.
Success is a smooth criminal
Too tricky to be caught.

Success is good trouble—

The force of the punch in the struggle
Between liberty and chains,
Brawns and brains,
The hunger pains of
The unsatiated soul—

Success is not a goal.

It is the fire within

The heart of a man that produces the win.

Future

Oh, how I wish they would never end:
The memories that I made with my friends.

I'd give anything to stop the close
Of the gates of love like a wilting rose.

To prevent the soldiers' of serenity their halt,
I would enter chaos' vault.

But I should be the one to know

That all good things must come and go;

Every now and again memories will rise
Like dead fish in a sea of lies,

Yet be aware they'll leave your hand
Like a vessel of flowing sand,

And memories, be careful how you use,
For only the future's yours to choose.

Grandmother

To be grand is to be full of awe and wonder
Like the roaring sound of thunder,

And what does it mean to be a mother?

To have cared for someone like no other.

When you put the two together, you get someone
Whose love has shown and deeds have done

What no other can do the same
Because Grandmother is her name.

School

Why do we attend?
We attend because we seek to mend
Our lives, our minds, our hearts, our souls—
In place of ignorance
We set goals.
Why do we attend?
Cuz books—they lend
A new reality;
When we read them
We find freedom—
New mentalities
Why do we attend?
We attend because we seek to fend
Off the hate, the lies,
The fate we try
Just to defend
Is the simple reason why we attend.

Oops

Not all poems have to rhyme—
Rhyming's not always on theme.
Hah! You thought I was gonna say "time"?
Dang it! I've created an ABAB rhyme scheme...

Graduation

You morph and grow through your school days.
Some things leave you; others stay.

It can sometimes feel like you've been remade,
And your life comes full circle in 8th grade.

Nostalgia strikes you in heaping waves;
It's a time to trail again the paths you've paved.

For a final time, you stroll the courts, watching the children play.
You pause, chuckle, and think to yourself: "I was once that way."

You admire the photos hanging on the school's entrance wall.
You think, "Will I exist only here to future kids who walk these halls?"

As you hand in your final tests, you look back on your academic path.
You feel accomplished, but, it's over? I'm almost wanting more math!

And as you walk your final steps, you know you've taken charge; the most beautiful theft.
So you cry a little, smile, and turn your tassel to the left.

Rubicon

Well, here we are, I guess—
At the point of no return.
I knew right from wrong no less,
Yet I could not discern.

There were two one-way flights to take,
And told which one to go,
I chose a different flight to make
And thought it wouldn't show.

But now, at the point of no return, I reside.
And if I could get back, I'd learn
To listen to the voice inside.

But here I am, at the point of no return.

Broken

How does it feel to be
The 4th Wall?
Not a character
Nor a spectator,
But the screen.
They disengage because the 4th Wall is
uncomfortable to break.

With a dream,
You ache—
You play their movie's scene—
You sit there with a frown,
Just waiting to be seen

Lest, the actors ignore you,
And audience looks past you.

What happens to the 4th Wall?

If not broken,

It goes black.

So break the 4th Wall—

Invite it to act.
Let spectators gaze its beauty,
And let no 4th Wall remain.
Challenge the concentration gradient to which individuals have been commodified.
Affirm the free flow between the set and the theater—
The answer and the call—
Until no such distinction exists
And no such 4th Wall.

Mother

Motherhood is not willed nor forced—
Motherhood is earned.
Motherhood is not instinctual—
Motherhood is learned.

The state or quality of being with child
Does not make a woman a Mother.

"Mother" is not an addition to a woman's name
But a new title,

For to become a Mother
She must give herself up—
Pour herself into her child;

She will never be the same,
For her child is now her world.

What does mother mean?

Mother means:

She has wrought greatness;
She has brought love.

Wise as a serpent;
Gentle as a dove.
Mother is my advocate;
Mother is my power.
Hard as an ox;
Peaceful as a flower.

Feeling

Love is not produced by what I feel,
Rather born of unrelenting zeal—
Stored as a chemical in my alleles—
Love's the deal,
Not the seal;
It's not for show,
It's there to heal.
Love's not the hug,
But what's revealed
By the warmth it brings;
The song love sings
Longs not for things but
Raises a wind that, like divine wings,
Floats one from the trenches of sorrow
Into a new tomorrow.
Love does not borrow—
It lends.
Love is not a feeling,
For love cannot end.

Metamorphosis

Why does the caterpillar live in a cocoon
When it's preparing to change?

'Tis that the caterpillar is volatile during
metamorphosis,
And the likely outcome is such:
That, without the cocoon, he would risk being named
By something that will never touch
The gentle breeze of the midday sky

Without the cocoon, he mayhaps comply
With the voices that tell him he won't rule July.

The cocoon is indespensable,

For what is a Monarch that cannot fly?

Tell Me What I Need To Know Suite

In Cmaj7

A tribute to my late grandfather.

A Better Place

Every day he spoke yearningly with the ancestors
And now, he has finally met them
I can picture it now
In the morning he rises by the Baobab trees
He skates a mile against a gentle breeze
He's on his way to visit Aunt Eileen
As he enters her home he is overcome with a feeling of magenta
For he is pleasantly surprised
To see Great Grandpa Summers and Great Grandma Frances at the door—
Aunt Connie's beside them—
And Aunt Nansuliwa
And many, many more
They've thrown him a surprise party
To welcome him home
As he makes his way inside he sees what's on the stove
Lentils and VooDoo Greens
And as they sit and they eat
They are happy to be
All together once more
In the evening he skates through the inner city

And behind the corner store
He and Omar Wally have a smoke—
Share some jokes—
'Bout how this new life's much better than before
Then before bed he's off to the arts center
For there they've some stories to tell
On the dais is a brother who jumped off the Middle Passage boat
There's also a griot from many years ago
And perhaps Tupac or Nipsey Hussle
After the presentation he raps with them
And they preach their groove of peace and love
Then after it all he skates on home
And rests under the shade of the Baobab tree
Friends, I say all this to say
That while we grieve and mourn
He is where he's meant to be
Proudly blowing his horn

Tell Me What I Need To Know

My Grandpa had an opinion on just about everything
How do I know this?
Every Sunday morning I'd give him a ring
Well, not only I, but my Mom as well
Every Sunday morning was show and tell
What I mean by this is that he came prepared
My Grandpa had a script for every conversation
He'd quiz me on the colors
Then differential equations
Then he'd read a poem, just one—
Nah, probably two
But soon he'd surely ask me,
"Can I hear from you?"
Reciprocity was his groove
I'd mumble bout my day
Or competitive spoils
Then with the wisdom of the ancestors
He'd fertilize the soils
Of my mind, my heart, my soul
Bringing affirmation to my goals
Jesus, Buddah, and Muhammad
Were all the same person
He'd share the Seven Virtues of Ma'at
From the Kemetic peoples in Africa

Or, at least, his version
Now that was his word, but as he'd say,
Each generation got they own groove
Therefore he looked forward to Sunday
Cuz I reminded him of him
At a simpler time in life
I reminded him of him before he had PTSD
So as we celebrate my Grandpa
And who he sought to be
Let's enter the place he tried his whole life to return to
As his spirit is set free
Let's be the best version of ourselves in his honor
And from him we can learn to
Be cool, be smooth
Live by principles
That's the groove
Fall back on the creator
Let him tell us where we need to go
And perhaps we'll change our voicemails
To "Tell Me What I Need to Know"

Made in the USA
Columbia, SC
27 May 2025